THE MAKING OF EVANGELICALISM

THE MAKING OF EVANGELICALISM

From Revivalism to Politics and Beyond

Randall Balmer

BAYLOR UNIVERSITY PRESS

Cover Design by Zeal Design Studio
Cover Image © Pete Seaward Photography/Riser/Getty Images

Library of Congress Cataloging-in-Publication Data

Balmer, Randall Herbert.
  The making of evangelicalism : from revivalism to politics and beyond / Randall Balmer.
      p. cm.
  Includes bibliographical references (p.   ).
  ISBN 978-1-60258-243-9 (alk. paper)
  1. Evangelicalism--United States--History. 2. United States--Church history. I. Title.
  BR1642.U5B344 2009
  270.8'2--dc22
                                        2009033606

Printed in the United States of America on acid-free paper.

for Sara

CONTENTS

INTRODUCTION

One of the forbidden pleasures in which historians indulge from time to time is counterfactual speculation. What if Constantine had not seen a vision of the cross before the Battle of Milvian Bridge in 312? Or what if he had seen a vision of a different sort? Suppose a favorable wind off the coast of Ireland had not assisted the English navy in its engagement against the Spanish Armada in 1588. Would the Church of England eventually have been reabsorbed into the Roman Catholic Church? Would the Netherlands have remained Protestant? What if John Calvin had been trained as an artist or a merchant rather than as a lawyer?

More often than not such speculations are idle and not terribly productive. Events and circumstances unfold a certain way, and any attempt to suppose otherwise is simply a species of mental gymnastics. But occasionally the posing of a counterfactual hypothesis helps to frame the issue and to sharpen discussion. This book, although it aims to "tell it like it was," also provides ample opportunities to imagine a different course at various junctures or turning points.

The subject here is evangelicalism in North America, the vast and diverse religious movement that Richard Ostling, formerly of *Time* magazine, once referred to as "America's folk religion." And here, at the outset, is as good a place as any to dispense with the matter of definition. The term *evangelical*, at its root, refers to the gospel—the "good news"—of the New Testament and, more specifically, to the four evangelists: Matthew, Mark, Luke, and John. Martin Luther's "rediscovery of the gospel" in the sixteenth century gave the term *evangelical* an unmistakably Protestant cast; to this day, Protestant churches in Germany are called *Evangelische*.

As I will argue later, the American strain of evangelicalism is peculiarly, well, American, and it derived from the eighteenth-century confluence of three "P"s: Scots-Irish Presbyterianism, Continental Pietism, and the vestiges of New England Puritanism. Evangelicalism in America has evolved and mutated over the centuries—that, in fact, is the burden of this book—but it is still possible to identify some generic characteristics: an embrace of the Holy Bible as inspired and God's revelation to humanity, a belief in the centrality of a conversion or "born again" experience, and the impulse to evangelize or bring others to the faith.

As with any such generalizations, these characteristics can be qualified, and I hasten to add that other scholars of evangelicalism offer more detailed and technical definitions. But I stand by my functional, three-fold definition as a descriptor for this vast swath of American evangelicals. And it is important also to note that, within that definition—or, to change the metaphor, beneath that umbrella—there is great diversity: fundamentalists, pentecostals, holiness people, charismatics, the sanctified tradition, neoevangelicals, various ethnic groups, and on and on. Evangelicalism is anything but homogeneous—racially, theologically, or politically.

Nor is it static. The genius of evangelicalism throughout American history is its malleability and the uncanny knack of evangelical leaders to speak the idiom of the culture, whether embodied in the open-air preaching of George Whitefield in the eighteenth century, the democratic populism of Peter Cartwright and Charles Finney on the frontier, or the suburban, corporate-style megachurches of the twentieth century. Evangelicalism is always changing, adapting to new surroundings and fresh circumstances.

One of the reasons evangelicalism is so pliable is that, unlike other religious traditions, it is not (for the most part) bound by ecclesiastical hierarchies, creedal formulas, or liturgical rubrics. For many evangelicals, even the word *tradition* has a negative valence; it suggests a kind of stultifying, calcified rigor that somehow, evangelicals believe, inhibits a true and dynamic embrace of the faith. Evangelicals prefer innovation to tradition in their worship and piety, if not their theology—although there are plenty of examples of that, as this book will demonstrate. Evangelicals are willing, even eager, to experiment with new ideas, especially in the realm of communications, and they are not afraid to discard ideas that do not work. This ability to discern and to speak the cultural idiom lends an unmistakably populist cast to evangelicalism in America. It also gives rise to a kind of cult of novelty.

★ ★ ★

Several times in its history, evangelicalism has faced transitional moments when the stakes were considerably higher than whether to jettison the organ for a praise band or do away with the wooden pulpit in favor of a plexiglass one. In the age of the Awakenings—the First Great Awakening and the Second Great Awakening—evangelicals dramatically revised their soteriology (theology of salvation). Although there were principled reasons for this shift, a web of demographic, sociological, and political changes must also be considered. What emerged early in the nineteenth century was a theology that fit the temper of the times, an assurance to people who had only recently taken their *political* destiny into their own hands that they controlled their *religious* destiny as well.

These early nineteenth-century evangelicals, it turned out, believed not only in the perfectibility of individuals but in the perfectibility of society itself, so they set about the enterprise of constructing a millennial kingdom here on earth and, more particularly, here in America. This ideology of postmillennialism—Jesus will return to earth *after* his followers had ushered in a millennial age of righteousness—animated various efforts of social amelioration all aimed at reforming society according to the norms of godliness. By the waning decades of the nineteenth century, however, in the face of urbanization, industrialization, and the influx of non-Protestant immigrants, evangelicals faced a second quandary: retain their vision of social reform or adopt an alternative theology, something called dispensational premillennialism, that would effectively absolve them from the task of improving society.

Following the shift in the understanding salvation between the First and Second Great Awakenings and the transition from postmillennialism to premillennialism, the third turning point for evangelicals followed inexorably from the second and had the effect of deepening evangelicalism's alienation from the broader society. The adoption of premillennialism late in the nineteenth century, a theology of despair, had turned evangelicals inward as they felt more and more estranged from the dominant culture. The construction of the evangelical subculture after the Scopes trial of 1925 and throughout the middle decades of the twentieth century provided evangelicals with their own constellation of congregations, denominations, mission societies, publishing houses, Bible camps, institutes, colleges, and seminaries. This insular world, a refuge from the depredations of the larger culture, protected evangelicals—and especially their children—from contamination. But it came at the price of almost total segregation from the outside world.

Paradoxically, the maturation of those institutions associated with the evangelical subculture by the 1970s provided the platform for evangelical reengagement with the broader society, the final turning point. The initial, albeit tentative, embrace of Jimmy Carter, a Southern Baptist Sunday school teacher, realigned evangelicalism with the political and social agenda of antebellum evangelicals, who invariably took the part of those on the margins of society. But a radical turnabout late in the 1970s shifted evangelicals away from their roots and into the ambit of right-wing political conservatism.

*   *   *

Four turning points. Four critical junctures in the formation of American evangelicalism. Four times when, in Robert Frost's memorable words, "two roads diverged in a yellow wood." Each of these junctures—the transition from Calvinist to Arminian theology in the embrace of revivalism, the shift from postmillennialism to premillennialism, the retreat into a subculture, and the rise of the Religious Right—invites counterfactual speculation. What if evangelicals had gone another way, had taken a different road back there in Robert Frost's woods? Might history have been different? Might evangelicals have been more faithful to the gospel they espouse had they chosen a different course?

At one level, as I suggested earlier, such ruminations constitute idle speculation. The past is past, water under the bridge. There is nothing we can do about it. But at another level, these lessons from the past can guide us into the future. "Those who cannot remember the past," the historian George Santayana warned us, "are condemned to repeat it."

It won't surprise you to learn that I believe evangelicals now, early in the twenty-first century, face another fork in the road. The election of Barack Obama on November 4, 2008, dealt a mortal blow to the Religious Right, although it will continue to thrash about for awhile. It is now possible to offer at least a preliminary assessment of the thirty-year history of this movement, one that dramatically reshaped the political landscape of the United States. And it is also possible to ask what effect this foray into a particular form of political activism had not only on the nation but on the nature and character of evangelicalism itself. Where do we go from here?

These are questions I mean to raise at the conclusion of this book, as evangelicals face still another critical juncture in their long and colorful history. But first, a look at the past.

1

THE AGE OF REVIVALS AND THE FIRST AMENDMENT

᛭

With the possible exception of the Second Great Awakening, no event in American religious history was more formative than the First Great Awakening, a massive revival of religion that swept through the Atlantic colonies in the middle decades of the eighteenth century. This Great Awakening reconfigured religious life in the colonies, and it introduced to American society a peculiar strain of evangelicalism that remains America's folk religion to this day. The Great Awakening featured such itinerant preachers as James Davenport, Gilbert Tennent, George Whitefield, and Andrew Crosswell, who articulated their evangelical message to receptive audiences, and it also showcased the intellectual gifts of Jonathan Edwards, who emerged as the principal theologian and apologist for the revival.

Edwards was a grandson of the estimable Solomon Stoddard, known (not affectionately) to Puritans in Boston as the "pope of the Connecticut Valley." Edwards's father, Timothy Edwards, was also a Congregationalist minister, and young Jonathan, a precocious and intellectually curious child, prepared to take up the family business. He graduated from Yale College at the age of seventeen and stayed an additional two years to study theology. After a brief and unremarkable stint as pastor of a Presbyterian congregation in New York City, Edwards returned to Yale as tutor in 1723, serving effectively as head of the institution in the confusing aftermath of the Anglican Apostasy, when the rector of the Congregationalist school, Timothy Cutler, and several tutors converted to the Church of England.

Edwards stayed at Yale for two years before accepting a call as assistant pastor to Stoddard, his grandfather, in Northampton, Massachusetts; he then succeeded to the pulpit at Stoddard's death in 1729. As early as the 1690s, contemporaneous with accounts from Gulliam Bertholf, a Pietist preacher in New Jersey, Stoddard had been reporting "harvests" among his congregations, by which he meant stirrings of religious revival. Stoddard's detractors in Boston were skeptical, in part because they did not care for Stoddard's theological innovations regarding the Lord's Supper, which he treated as a converting ordinance and not one reserved for those who were demonstrably regenerate.

During the winter of 1734–1735, a revival of religion swept through Northampton, during Edwards's tenure as pastor. Three hundred people were added to the congregation, and religion, according to Edwards, became the dominant topic of conversation among the townspeople. After the revival waned somewhat, the fires were rekindled with the visit of George Whitefield in 1740, during his tour of the Atlantic colonies. By this time the revival was widespread, a phenomenon known to contemporaries as a "great and general awakening" and to historians as the Great Awakening.

The Great Awakening reshaped American society in important ways. In New England especially, and to a lesser degree in the Middle Colonies and in the Chesapeake, the revival fractured the unity of colonial society. Countless New England towns bear witness to the effects of the revival. The village green in New Haven, Connecticut, for instance, has the Old Light Congregational church at its center, flanked by the New Light (revivalist) congregation on one side and the Episcopal church on the other. The revival divided congregations and communities, but it also disrupted the social fabric of colonial America, the halcyon vision of the Puritans where church and state were both coterminous and mutually reinforcing.

The Awakening also introduced evangelicalism into American society; more accurately, it created a strain of evangelicalism unique to North America, unlike previous iterations coming out of the Protestant Reformation. I generally refer to the ingredients in this mixture as the three "P"s: the remnants of New England Puritanism, Pietism from the Continent, and Scots-Irish Presbyterianism. The confluence of these streams during the years of the Great Awakening produced evangelicalism in America, and to this day evangelicalism retains some of the characteristics of each: the obsessive introspection of Puritanism, the doctrinal precisionism of the Presbyterians, and the warmhearted spiritual ardor of the Pietists. Although, as we will see, the Second Great Awakening utterly recast evangelical theology, the essential elements of the three "P"s can be discerned to the present.

★ ★ ★

Other forces were at work that abetted the success of the Great Awakening, factors that would have a profound impact on evangelicalism throughout American history. The arrival of Whitefield signaled an important shift in the tactics of revivalism. Whitefield, an Anglican clergyman, had been trained in the London theater, so he understood how to modulate his voice and pause for dramatic effect. In the context of colonial America, in a society that had no theatrical tradition, Whitefield's stentorian preaching was inordinately successful. Contemporaries said that he could bring tears to your eyes simply by saying "Mesopotamia," and as even the hardened religious skeptic Benjamin Franklin could attest, Whitefield was a persuasive orator. Franklin's famous account of Whitefield's visit to Society Hill in Philadelphia stands as a monument to Whitefield's effectiveness. Franklin admired Whitefield as a friend, though he had no time for his religion or for Whitefield's pet project, an orphanage in Georgia, which Franklin regarded as too remote to do much good. Early on in Whitefield's oration, Franklin recognized that he was heading toward an appeal for funds. Franklin resolved not to give anything, then, after a time, decided to surrender the coppers in his pocket. Another rhetorical flourish and Franklin consented to give the silver, and Whitefield concluded so gloriously that Franklin entirely emptied his pockets into the collection plate, gold and all.

Franklin's account of Whitefield's visit to Society Hill also included his careful calculations that Whitefield's voice could be heard by ten thousand people. This brings us to another observation about evangelical innovations during the Great Awakening: popular appeal. As Whitefield perambulated along the Atlantic seaboard, he would often ask to use the local meetinghouse. But as word of Whitefield's success began to circulate, many of the settled clergy, fearing for their livelihoods, denied him access. Undaunted, Whitefield took his message directly to the people, preaching in the open air in the fields or on the village greens. By circumventing the clergy and the established churches, Whitefield and his evangelical confrérés displayed the knack for populist communications that would become characteristic of evangelicalism to the present day. From the open-air preaching of Whitefield and a passel of itinerant preachers to the circuit riders and the colporteurs of the nineteenth century to the urban evangelism of Billy Sunday and Billy Graham in the twentieth century, evangelicals have always understood the importance of communicating directly with the masses, absent the niceties of ecclesiastical and denominational forms or even sanctified venues.

So influential was Whitefield's extemporaneous preaching that even Jonathan Edwards struggled to keep pace with the changing times and circumstances of the

Great Awakening. If you visit the Beineke Library at Yale and ask to see the originals of Edwards's sermons, you'll notice that they are palm-sized folios stitched into a booklet; Edwards scholars speculate, plausibly, that Edwards concealed the text of his sermons in his hand in order to convey the impression that he was preaching extemporaneously, when in fact he was not. Itinerant preachers like Whitefield, on the other hand, had the advantage of being able to repeat the same sermons time after time to changing audiences, thereby perfecting their styles of delivery—an advantage, as Franklin noted, denied to the settled clergy, who had to come up with fresh material every week.

★ ★ ★

Aside from the rhetorical advantages enjoyed by Whitefield and others, itinerancy had an enormous effect on religion in the eighteenth century. It provided religious choices for the populace, options other than the established Congregationalist churches in New England, the Church of England in the South, or the traditionalist Dutch Reformed and Anglican churches in the Middle Colonies. The presence of itinerants forced the settled clergy to compete in what was emerging as a religious marketplace. Clergy could no longer rely solely on their sinecures; they had to maintain a rapport with their congregants for the simple reason that their congregants had other ecclesiastical options, especially with the emergence of the Baptists in New England and the Chesapeake, the Pietists and the Presbyterians in the Middle Colonies, and various religious "entrepreneurs" in Pennsylvania and the South.

A kind of religious populism emerged in the eighteenth century that obtains to this day and can be seen most clearly in the televangelists and the megachurches. The televangelists, moreover, have solved forever the great riddle of itinerancy throughout American history: through the miracle of electronic communications, the itinerant preacher, always an insurgent presence, can now be everywhere at once. But the ubiquity of itinerant preachers and the emergence of religious options in the eighteenth century had another important effect: the absence of anticlericalism. The caricature of the besotted, overweight, indulgent vicar or parson—so common in British humor—has no real counterpart here in America. The reason, I believe, is simple. In a free marketplace of religion, clerics cannot afford to be complacent or negligent toward their congregants. They must always be conscious of popular sentiment—a two-edged sword, no doubt, because populism can always degenerate into demagoguery or into a theology of the lowest common denominator. But itinerancy and the religious marketplace ensure that religious leaders are always attentive to popular sentiment, and they ignore it at their peril.

Itinerancy and the free marketplace for religion also figured into the First Amendment proscriptions against religious establishment. Roger Williams, Puritan minister in Salem, Massachusetts, ran afoul of the Puritan authorities shortly after his arrival in the New World in 1631. Specifically, Williams feared the deleterious effects on the faith if church and state were too closely aligned. In his words, he sought to protect the "garden of the church" from the "wilderness of the world" by means of a "wall of separation," and it is important here to remember that the Puritans did not share our romantic visions about wilderness; for them, the wilderness was dark and forbidding, a place of danger where evil lurked. Williams's notion of church-state separation challenged the orthodoxy of the Puritan experiment, and for his troubles Williams was banished from the colony. He proceeded to Rhode Island, which the Puritans came to regard as a cesspool of religious heresy, and founded there a haven of religious toleration, which guaranteed liberty of individual conscience and the separation of church and state.

While in Rhode Island, Williams also founded the Baptist tradition in America, a tradition that, until very recently, enshrined two notions: adult or believer's baptism (as opposed to infant baptism) and the separation of church and state. Williams's ideas about disestablishment were picked up by such evangelical leaders as Isaac Backus and John Leland, and one of the great paradoxes of the eighteenth century is that these evangelicals allied themselves with Enlightenment types to press for religious disestablishment in the new nation.

This alliance of strange bedfellows produced the First Amendment to the United States Constitution, which reads in part: "Congress shall make no law respecting an establishment of religion, or prohibiting the free exercise thereof." It codified the free marketplace of religion that had been the configuration by default in many of the colonies. It ensured that Americans would never have to deal with the miserable effects of religious establishment, effects that many of the founders knew all too well from their experience of Great Britain and the Continent. While it is probably true that Thomas Jefferson wanted to maintain that "wall of separation" in order to protect the fragile new government from religious factionalism, whereas Williams wanted the "wall of separation" to preserve the integrity of the faith, the happy consequence of the First Amendment is that both sides benefited handsomely. Religious faith has flourished in America as nowhere else precisely because the government has (for the most part, at least) stayed out of the religion business. At the same time, allowing religious groups to function freely in the marketplace of popular discourse has tended to dissipate voices of political dissent, just as James Madison predicted in *Federalist Number 10*.

The First Amendment has allowed religious entrepreneurs, from Mother Ann Lee and Joseph Smith to Mary Baker Eddy and Elijah Muhammad, to peddle their wares in the free marketplace of American religion. But no group has functioned more effectively in this marketplace than evangelicals themselves. Evangelicals understand almost instinctively how to speak the idiom of the culture, whether it be Whitefield's extemporaneous, open-air preaching, the circuit riders blanketing the South in the antebellum period, or the curricula and the entertainment of the megachurches, exquisitely attuned to the tastes of suburbanites in the late twentieth century. No religious movement in American history has benefited more from religious disestablishment, which makes the persistent attempts on the part of the Religious Right to eviscerate the First Amendment utterly confounding. Why would any evangelical seek to compromise the very basis for the popularity of his faith?

Perhaps we can bring some clarity to the issue with a counterfactual proposal: suppose the founders had followed the historical precedent of at least a dozen centuries and established a religion for the new nation. Suppose, in other words, that the First Amendment contained only the provisions of the second clause, guaranteeing freedom of speech and the press, and no proscription against religious establishment? What would religion in America look like today?

We do not have to search very far. In Great Britain, the Church of England, the established religion, draws less than three percent of the population to its Sunday services. Several years back, the bishops of the state Lutheran church in Sweden, seeing the benefits of disestablishment, successfully petitioned the Swedish parliament to rescind the Lutherans' establishment status. The results were so impressive that the Lutheran bishops in Norway also asked to be disestablished.

The First Amendment has ensured a salubrious religious culture in the United States, one unmatched anywhere in the world. If the founders had not stood up to those who wanted to designate Christianity as the religion of the new nation, the religious environment would most likely look very different, anemic in comparison with the religious vitality we see both today and throughout American history.

★ ★ ★

If the First Great Awakening introduced evangelicalism into the American context, the Second Great Awakening in the decades surrounding the turn of the nineteenth century reshaped the movement in profound ways. Although some of the changes were tactical, the most dramatic shift was theological.

One of the first things I learned in my study of American church history was the profound difference in the theological underpinnings of the First and the Second Great Awakenings, as reflected in the theological dispositions of their respective apologists, Jonathan Edwards and Charles Grandison Finney. Edwards's history of the revival, published in 1737, remains a classic statement of a Calvinist approach to revival. The title, in many ways, tells you all you need to know about Edwards's understanding of the remarkable events in Northampton: *A Faithful Narrative of a Surprising Work of God*. It was Edwards's clear understanding that the revival in Northampton was a gracious visitation of the divine; there was nothing that Edwards had done to prompt such a visitation, much less to merit it. God, in his wisdom and infinite mercy, through the agency of the Holy Spirit, had chosen to work his regenerative wonders among the people of Northampton without regard to the merit or the efforts of either the congregants or their minister. In so doing, God had demonstrated his unfathomable mercy for all to see.

Charles Finney, on the other hand, had a very different understanding of revival. Finney famously declared in his *Lectures on Revivals of Religion* that revival was "the work of man." Finney, born in Warren, Connecticut, and trained as a lawyer, had a religious conversion in 1821 and determined that he had been given "a retainer from the Lord Jesus Christ to plead his cause." The St. Lawrence presbytery licensed him to preach in 1823 and ordained him the following year. He began preaching in upstate New York under the auspices of the Female Missionary Society of the Western District in 1824.

Early in his career, Finney harbored doubts about Calvinism, not so much on theological as on pragmatic grounds; Finney was convinced that Calvinistic determinism simply did not lend itself to revival. Instead, he preached that by the mere exercise of volition anyone could repent of sin and thereby claim salvation. Contrary to the Calvinist and Edwardsean doctrine of election, the notion that God alone determined who was or was not part of the elect and thereby regenerate, Finney preached that salvation was available to all; it required merely an assent on the part of the individual.

Finney's soteriology elevated persuasion to new heights of importance. If only the preacher could convince sinners to repent and to accept salvation for themselves, then revival would be assured—no need any longer to wait for the mysterious movings of the Holy Spirit or the even more elusive effectual "call" of Calvinist election. In order to help things along, Finney promoted what he called "new measures," a set of strategic initiatives to engender revivals: protracted meetings, the use of advertising, allowing women to testify at religious gatherings, and the "anxious bench" or "mourner's bench," where those deliberating their eternal fates could come for counseling.

It does not take much imagination to recognize that these "new measures" have become part of the fabric of modern evangelism, as witnessed by Billy Graham crusades in the twentieth century; Graham's call for his auditors to "make a decision for Christ" came straight from Finney's playbook. But the familiarity of these tactics tends to disguise their revolutionary character in the early decades of the nineteenth century. Whereas Jonathan Edwards had understood revival as "a surprising work of God," Finney described it as "the work of man." Therein lies an utter reconfiguration of evangelical theology, from the Calvinist orientation of the First Great Awakening to the Arminian theology (named for Jacobus Arminius) of the Second Great Awakening, which also had strong affinities with Wesleyanism, the theology of John Wesley.

Why did Finney's formulation take hold so rapidly in the early decades of the nineteenth century? Several reasons. First, Finney's new theology fit the temper of the times. Among a people who had only recently taken their *political* destiny into their own hands, Finney assured them that they controlled their *religious* destiny as well. At least as popularly understood, salvation was no longer an anxiety-laden process of waiting to determine whether or not you were among the elect; now, in Finney's scheme, an individual could initiate the process by means of volition. If you want to be saved, all you need to do is decide to be saved. No need any longer to sweat through the elaborate Calvinist soteriology as propagated in deadly detail by such Puritan divines as William Perkins and Jonathan Edwards.

Finney's formula had obvious appeal in the new nation, especially among a people inebriated with self-determinism. And to this day we Americans cherish this notion of rugged individualism and control of our own destinies. The Edwardsean theology of salvation and revival seems stilted and confining, whereas Finney's is supple and accommodating.

Finney's formulaic approach to revival also fit the social and economic circumstances of the nineteenth century. In an age of nascent industrialization and scientific rationalism, Finney's notion that revival was available simply by following an ordered set of steps and observing certain conventions worked very well. To hear Finney tell it, all you needed to do was combine the elements—advertising, protracted meetings, women's testimony, anxious bench—like you would in a chemical formula, and revival would be assured. And in an age of nascent industrialization and one increasingly enamored of technology, Finney's formulaic approach to revival matched the cultural moment. By the time that B. W. Gorham published his *Camp Meeting Manual* in 1854, the business of revivalism had been reduced to a science; Gorham, enlarging on Finney's prescriptions, dictated everything from locations to publicity strategies to instructions on how to construct the tents—all in the effort to guarantee a successful camp meeting.

The twentieth-century iteration of Gorham's *Camp Meeting Manual* was the Billy Graham Evangelistic Association and especially its elaborate preparations for Graham's crusades. The well-oiled corporate machinery of the

BGEA was honed to utter perfection and serves as a model of efficiency. Once a venue had been chosen for a revival (at least three years before the event itself), the organization swept into motion, calibrating everything from site selection and religious alliances to music programs and press coverage. Nothing was left to chance, and all contingencies were accounted for down to the tiniest detail. Far from relying on "a surprising work of God," modern revivalism owes an incalculable debt to the formulaic strategies of Charles Finney and B. W. Gorham.

The overriding genius of Finney and the theological innovations he introduced to American evangelicalism is that they suited perfectly the *Zeitgeist* and the emerging self-perception of Americans. Finney's Arminianism comported well with the storied rugged individualism that so shapes American identity, and his insistence that we control our own religious destiny was far more congenial to the American illusion of self-determinism than the arcane Calvinist doctrines of foreknowledge, predestination, and election.

★ ★ ★

After the Second Great Awakening and the theological innovations of Charles Finney, evangelical theology would never be the same. Reformed theology made one last, albeit sustained, stand in the person of Charles Hodge and his nineteenth-century colleagues at Princeton Theological Seminary. But theirs was a forlorn and hopeless battle, one fought increasingly on the ramparts of a hyper-rationalism that owed as much to the Enlightenment as it did to Calvin or even to historic Christianity.

In recent years, Calvinists have tried to stage a comeback on two fronts, both theological and historical. Various evangelical historians have tried to assert that the theological essence of evangelicalism is Reformed, not Wesleyan or Arminian, and that the true progenitors of contemporary evangelicalism are the Princetonians, not the Finneyites. Some denominations, such as the Southern Baptist Convention and the denomination of my childhood, the Evangelical Free Church, have even tried to recast themselves in the tradition of Reformed theology rather than Arminian theology. The Free Church, for instance, a denomination with deep roots in Scandinavian Pietism and strong affinities with Arminianism, has, through the agency of its flagship seminary, Trinity Evangelical Divinity School, laid claims to being Calvinist. Among other consequences, a denomination that ordained women in its early years now frowns on the ordination of women.

What is the attraction of Calvinism to contemporary evangelicals? I think their attempt to recast themselves in the Reformed tradition is a reaction, at least in part, to the runaway success of pentecostalism in the twentieth century. That is, many evangelicals, especially those associated with seminaries, believe that Calvinism is more intellectually respectable and theologically rigorous than Wesleyanism or Arminianism, and so they have taken great pains to associate themselves with the Reformed tradition in an attempt to trade on what they perceive as its intellectual heft—even to the point of denying their own historical and theological roots.

Such efforts come largely to naught, however, at the grass roots. Finney's pragmatism and his brand of Arminianism carried the day among evangelicals—in the antebellum period and ever since. At least as understood at the popular level, the revivalist's plea to come to Jesus or Billy Graham's invitation to "make a decision for Christ" makes little sense in the Calvinist and Edwardsean scheme of revival, where even the repentant sinner must await the visitation of grace. Finney assured all Americans that they controlled the mechanism of salvation, and the evangelical tradition has never been the same.

But it still would have foundered without the underpinnings of the First Amendment. Unbound by establishment status, and not compelled to compete against another religion that enjoyed establishment status, evangelicalism has competed freely in the American religious marketplace. And it has done so with intelligence, vigor, and savvy. From the extemporaneous oratory of George Whitefield to the organizational efficiency of Billy Graham, evangelicals have understood better than anyone else how to communicate to the masses. The message they propagate is simple, straightforward, and utterly indebted to Charles Finney. Come to Jesus. Make a decision for Christ. You control your own spiritual destiny.

And somewhere in the Presidents' Plot of the Princeton, New Jersey, cemetery, Jonathan Edwards, theologian of the First Great Awakening, is spinning in his grave.

2

THE TRANSITION
FROM POSTMILLENNIALISM
TO PREMILLENNIALISM

᪥

Charles Finney's theological revolution had repercussions for evangelicals far beyond the arcane arena of
soteriology, the doctrine of salvation. At least as popularly
understood, Finney's Arminianism assured Americans
that they controlled their own religious destiny, that they
could initiate the process of salvation simply by exercise of
volition. Finney's declaration that revival was "the work
of man" led to a codification and a routinization of evangelism. Beginning with Finney and extending to B. W.
Gorham's *Camp Meeting Manual* and to Billy Graham and
various revivalists of the twentieth century, the enterprise
of revival became formulaic, almost mechanistic. As long
as you followed certain conventions, Finney and others
promised, revival would ensue.

The social implications of Finney's ideas were even more profound. If individuals controlled their ultimate destinies, surely it did not require much of a leap to suppose that their actions here on earth could affect the temporal realm as well. And the aggregate actions of believers could bring about monumental changes in society.

Aside from the individual empowerment implicit in Arminian soteriology, another theological discipline figured into antebellum evangelicalism: postmillennialism. Throughout church history, generations of theologians have puzzled over the prophetic passages of the Bible, from Isaiah and Ezekiel and Daniel in the Hebrew Bible to Revelation and 2 Thessalonians in the New Testament. Jesus himself suggested some sort of apocalyptic development within a generation, and the book of Revelation contains all manner of images and events that should or should not be interpreted literally and should or should not be understood as prophetic. What do we make of the mark of the beast or the emergence of the antichrist? Revelation 20 talks about a millennium, one thousand years of godly rule. What does that mean? When will it occur, now or later? Ann Lee of the Shakers, for example, taught that the millennium was already in place and that this new age dictated that women and men should no longer engage in sexual relations, whereas John Humphrey Noyes of the Oneida Community believed that the millennial age loosened the bonds of exclusivity in marriage, thereby allowing for sexual license.

Theologians over the centuries have disagreed, sometimes spectacularly, over the meaning of these apocalyptic passages, but by the nineteenth century two broad streams of interpretation had emerged: premillennialism and post-millennialism. Although the multitude of interpretations and the infinity of nuances make generalizations difficult, those who numbered themselves premillennialists believed that Jesus would return to earth to take his followers out of the world, an event known as the rapture. Those left behind would face hardship and judgment in a period known as the tribulation. Eventually, however, Jesus and his followers would return to earth for the millennium, the one thousand years of righteous rule, before the culmination of time in the last judgment. Postmillennialists, on the other hand, held that Jesus would return to earth after the millennium, that there would be no disruption between this temporal age and the onset of the millennium.

The sequence here is crucial. Premillennialists believe that Jesus will return *before* the millennium (hence *pre-millennialism*), whereas *post*millennialists hold that Jesus will return *after* the millennium, the one thousand years of righteousness. Although this may appear to be a recondite doctrinal debate, the unfortunate detritus of people with too much time on their hands, this distinction has had enormous repercussions for the ways that evangelicals approach society. If you believe that Jesus will return after the millennium with no disruption in the advance of time, the corollary is that it is incumbent on believers themselves to construct the righteous kingdom. If, on the other hand, your reading of scripture leads you to believe that Jesus will come for his followers before the millennial age, then the onset of the millennial kingdom will come later in the apocalyptic calendar, thereby absolving believers from responsibility for bringing about the millennial kingdom in this age.

* * *

This is exactly what played out among evangelicals in the nineteenth century. Given the Arminian theology that dominated the Second Great Awakening—the doctrine that individuals could exercise their volition to initiate the salvation process—it should come as no surprise that the concomitant eschatology of the Second Awakening was postmillennialism, the notion that Jesus would return after the millennium. The corollary of postmillennialism was that believers bore the responsibility for bringing on the millennium by dint of their own efforts. Those who had appropriated salvation for themselves now looked to broaden their efforts and inaugurate the kingdom of God on earth, more particularly here in America.

And that is precisely what they set about to do. The Second Great Awakening unleashed a reforming zeal unmatched in the annals of American history. Evangelical converts, convinced of their mandate to usher in the millennium, set about to purge society of its ills. They recognized that slavery was an abomination and inconsistent with a millennial society, so they organized to abolish it. They were part of the temperance crusade, which in the nineteenth century was a progressive cause. They joined with Horace Mann and others in support of public education, known as common schools in the nineteenth century; many of the early leaders of public education were Protestant clergy. Part of the rationale for public schools was to advance the lot of children of the less fortunate and also to provide a foundation for democracy by allowing children of different backgrounds to learn from one another in the classroom and on the playground and get along with one another with at least a measure of comity. Evangelicals opened female seminaries to raise the literacy rates among women to a level of parity with men by the middle of the century, and they sought to advance the rights of women generally, including the right to vote.

All of these initiatives were directed (at least in part) toward the goal of constructing the kingdom of God on earth. To take another example, the redoubtable Lyman Beecher was horrified when Aaron Burr, vice president of the United States, killed Alexander Hamilton in a duel in Weehawken, New Jersey, on the morning of July 11, 1804. (Dick Cheney was not the first sitting vice president in American history to shoot a man!) Beecher decided that the barbaric practice of dueling was not a fixture of the millennial kingdom, so he launched a campaign, ultimately successful, to outlaw dueling as part of his efforts to inaugurate the millennial age.

Much of this reforming energy unleashed by the Second Great Awakening came from women. Finney had authorized women to participate more fully in religious gatherings than they ever had before (with the possible exception of the first century), and evangelical women, many of them freed by nascent industrialization and middle-class privilege from the drudgery of subsistent living, devoted their considerable energies to social activism. These evangelical women served as tireless foot soldiers in the campaign to usher in the millennial age.

America would never be the same. Postmillennial evangelicals in the antebellum period, convinced that they could bring about the millennium by their own efforts, energized social reform and utterly reshaped American society. The power of their arguments and the urgency of their activism led Americans to the brink of irreparable schism and the Civil War.

★ ★ ★

With the onset of war, however, the postmillennial optimism of antebellum evangelicals began to fade. The carnage of the war itself represented a disappointment; northern evangelicals hoped that the moral clarity of their case against slavery, combined with divine favor, would bring the conflict speedily to a conclusion. Victory, however, proved elusive. But there were other factors at work in American society as well, factors that called the entire postmillennial enterprise into question.

The character of American society over the course of the nineteenth century was reshaped by both industrialization and urbanization. Industrialization, beginning with the textile mills of New England, changed forever both the work and domestic patterns of Americans. Employment in the mills transported adults out of the home and into the workplace, thereby altering the dynamics of the family. Men, working now beyond the ken of church and home, began to socialize in networks with fellow workers; their wives increasingly socialized with one another and in circles defined by religious affiliations. Men came to be seen as "worldly," an impression that lent urgency to the Second Great Awakening in boom areas like Rochester, New York, but that also fed what scholars have called the "feminization" of American religion, the shift of spiritual responsibility from men to women.

If industrialization altered American domestic life by changing patterns of socializing, the accompanying demographic phenomenon of urbanization similarly shook the theological understanding of America's evangelicals. The move to the cities exposed evangelicals to a different world from the relatively bucolic and small-town life that had prevailed in the earlier decades of the nineteenth century. Add to that the changing ethnic and religious composition of Americans, and evangelicals suddenly felt their hegemonic hold over American society slipping away.

Put in its starkest terms, the teeming, squalid ghettoes of the lower east side of Manhattan, festering with labor unrest, no longer resembled the precincts of Zion that postmillennial evangelicals had envisioned earlier in the century. Immigrants, including Jews and Roman Catholics, most of whom did not share evangelical scruples about temperance, represented a threat to the millennial aspirations of American evangelicals. The world, at least as seen through the lens of the United States, was getting worse, not better. Righteousness, which was often confused with white, middle-class, Victorian ideals, had given way to wickedness: unemployment, filth, drunkenness, disease, and the corruption of urban political machines.

Faced with this wretchedness, American evangelicals looked to alter their eschatology. Postmillennial optimism about the advent of a millennial kingdom here in America no longer seemed appropriate, so evangelicals cast about for another interpretation of those biblical prophetic passages. They found an answer from an unlikely source, a former barrister and Anglican priest named John Nelson Darby, who had left the Church of England in 1831 for a small, Pietistic group called the Plymouth Brethren. Darby became enamored of a new hermeneutic of biblical interpretation called dispensationalism, or dispensational premillennialism.

Dispensationalism posited that all of human history could be divided into discrete ages (or dispensations) and that God had dealt differently with humanity in each of these dispensations. God had struck a particular deal, or covenant, with Adam, for instance, and another with Noah and Abraham and with the people of Israel. The present dispensation, Darby argued, called for the separation of true believers from nonbelievers in anticipation of the imminent, premillennial return of Jesus. In other words, Jesus may return at any moment, before the millennium, and the corollary of Darby's teaching was that those left behind at the rapture would face the judgment and the wrath of God. Indeed, Darby even insisted that the social degeneration apparent everywhere should be taken as evidence that Jesus would soon return to rescue believers out of this mess.

Darby came to North America to propagate these ideas, making seven visits between 1859 and 1874. He found there a receptive audience, and his scheme eventually caught the attention of such evangelical figures as Dwight L. Moody, A. J. Gordon, and James H. Brooks. Just as Finney's Arminianism suited the temper of the new nation, the pessimism implicit in Darbyism took hold among American evangelicals. Premillennialism, with its assertion that Jesus would return at any time, effectively absolved evangelicals of any responsibility for social reform. Dispensationalism taught that such efforts ultimately were unavailing.

For American evangelicals, part of the appeal of dispensationalism was its esoteric nature. Darby provided the Rosetta Stone for understanding the confusing and apparently contradictory prophecies in the Scriptures. Dispensationalism allowed evangelicals triumphantly to announce, in effect, that they had cracked the code. They understood the mind of God. Anyone who did not acknowledge this historic breakthrough was, by definition, benighted, and terrible judgment awaited them at the return of Jesus.

* * *

It is worth noting that not all nineteenth-century evangelicals fall into this tidy scheme of antebellum postmillennialists and postbellum premillennialists. William Miller, a farmer and biblical interpreter from Low Hampton, New York, believed that Jesus would return sometime in 1843 or 1844. Approximately fifty thousand followers were persuaded by his arcane calculations, and as the date approached they whipped themselves into a frenzy of anticipation. When Jesus failed to materialize as predicted on October 22, 1844, Miller's followers returned home disappointed, and this event (or non-event) is known to this day among Adventists as the Great Disappointment.

If the Millerites represented the premillennial exception in antebellum evangelicalism, the most notable exception to premillennialism among evangelicals in the latter part of the nineteenth century was the Salvation Army. Known originally as the Christian Mission when it was established in the slums of London in 1865, the Salvation Army, part of the holiness movement, retained its emphasis on social reform and social amelioration even after it arrived in the United States in 1880. The Salvation Army, with its slum brigades, its street-corner preaching, and its battles against the systemic ills of the ghettoes, managed to retain its twin emphases on evangelism and social reform.

With their embrace of dispensationalism, however, evangelicals on the whole shifted their focus radically from social amelioration to individual regeneration. Having diverted their attention from the construction of the millennial realm, evangelicals concentrated on the salvation of souls and, in so doing, neglected reform efforts. "I look upon this world as a wrecked vessel," Moody famously declared. "God has given me a lifeboat and said, 'Moody, save all you can.'"

★ ★ ★

The social and demographic upheavals of the late nineteenth century mark the beginning of a great divide in American Protestantism. As evangelicals retreated into a theology of despair, one that essentially ceded the temporal world to Satan and his minions, other Protestants allied with the Progressive movement assumed the task of social amelioration. Led by such pastor-theologians as Washington

Gladden of Columbus, Ohio, and Walter Rauschenbusch in New York City, aided by such theorists as Richard T. Ely of the University of Wisconsin, and popularized by Charles M. Sheldon's novel *In His Steps*, the Social Gospel emerged to take up the cause of social reform. Although they seldom invoked the language of postmillennialism, the proponents of the Social Gospel, also known as Social Christianity or Christian Socialism, sought to make this world a better place, especially for the wretched of society. They believed that Jesus redeemed not merely sinful individuals but sinful social institutions as well.

To that end, the Social Gospel, working arm in arm with political Progressives, pushed for child-labor laws and for the six-day workweek. They sought to discredit and to destroy the urban political machines by exposing their corruption. They advocated the rights of workers to organize, and they sought to blunt the effects of predatory capitalism. At the same time that evangelicals were retreating into their otherworldy reverie, looking for the imminent return of Jesus, the more theologically liberal Social Gospel advocates sought to reform the present world to make it more nearly represent a godly society.

As the twentieth century progressed, these two streams of American Protestantism grew ever more divergent. Although the Social Gospel itself was popularly discredited by the Bolshevik Revolution of 1917 and the attendant rise of Communism, the ideas of Rauschenbusch resurfaced in the thought of Martin Luther King Jr. in the 1950s after King had encountered the Social Gospel in graduate school. Though the Social Gospel label had lost its allure, liberal Protestants continued to align themselves with the ideals of the Social Gospel, the mandate that the followers of Jesus bore responsibility for redressing the evils of society. As evident in the civil rights struggle, opposition to the war in Vietnam, support for the rights of women, and a sympathetic disposition toward immigrants and the poor, liberal Protestants have tried to retain the principles of the Social Gospel, which in turn reflects, at least dimly, the principles of nineteenth-century postmillennialism.

★　★　★

And what about the evangelicals, the other stream of American Protestantism? Throughout most of the twentieth century, at least until the rise of the Religious Right in the late 1970s, evangelicals clung to premillennialism and its emphasis on individual regeneration rather than social amelioration. They evinced little interest in social issues; this world, after all, was doomed and transitory. Politics itself was corrupt and corrupting, and many evangelicals did not even trouble themselves to vote. Jesus would appear at any moment to rescue them from the morass of the present world, so why invest any significant energies in making it a better place? With time so short, moreover, all resources—money, energy, personnel—should be deployed in the enterprise of evangelism and missions, bringing others into the kingdom of God in preparation for the end of time.

Fueled by dispensationalist ideology, evangelism and missionary efforts flourished among evangelicals in the early decades of the twentieth century—at a time when mainline Protestants, fraught with misgivings, were throttling back on missionary activity, especially after the *Re-Thinking Missions* report of 1932, which urged missionaries to be more attentive to the integrity of other cultures. Evangelism took many forms, from the vaudeville antics of Billy Sunday and the corporate efficiency of Billy Graham to the "Four Spiritual Laws" of Campus Crusade for Christ and the come-to-Jesus appeals of the televangelists. But the overriding focus of their efforts was individual redemption, not social action. When asked about reforming society, Graham would routinely respond that the only way to change society was "to change men's hearts," by which he meant that only the aggregate effect of individual conversions would bring about real reform.

Aside from the emphasis on personal evangelism and the neglect of social amelioration, what have been the effects of the evangelical shift from postmillennialism to premillennialism? I can think of two material consequences related to the evangelical penchant for dispensationalism. The first is lack of concern for the environment and the natural world. For much of the twentieth century, and even militantly so during the last several decades, evangelicals have been notoriously uninterested in environmental preservation. If Jesus is going to return soon to rescue the true believers and to unleash judgment on those left behind, why should we devote any attention whatsoever to care of the earth, which will soon be destroyed in the apocalypse predicted in the book of Revelation?

In recent decades, this premillennial disposition on the part of evangelicals combined with some blend of capitalism and libertarianism to produce a concoction even more hostile to environmental interests. This amalgam reached its apotheosis in the person of James G. Watt, an Assemblies of God layman and Ronald Reagan's secretary of the interior. Watt had been associated with the so-called Sagebrush Rebellion, a coalition of western ranchers who wanted to open more wilderness areas to development and who opposed any efforts to alter their favorable grazing rights on federal lands. After Reagan, who famously remarked that if you'd seen one redwood tree you'd seen them all, tapped Watt to be secretary of the interior, Watt remarked to stunned members of the House Interior Committee, "I don't know how many future generations we can count on before the Lord returns." Watt insisted in later years that he meant that environmental resources had to be husbanded long enough to last until the rapture, but his remark was widely interpreted as a justification for his lack of interest in environmental protection.

The second twentieth-century legacy of evangelical premillennialism is less pernicious but no less regrettable: bad religious architecture, sometimes spectacularly bad architecture. If Jesus is coming at any moment, why waste precious time and resources on fancy buildings? The unfortunate legacy of this attitude can be seen in evangelical church buildings and on countless Bible institute and Bible college campuses, where function does not merely triumph over form, it utterly obliterates it. Cinderblock and folding chairs would do just fine, and the theological disregard for the sacraments, so common among evangelicals, only exacerbated this tendency to neglect aesthetics.

To be fair, another factor contributed to the bad architecture, namely a lack of resources. Following the fundamentalist-modernist controversies of the 1920s, many evangelicals felt duty-bound to secede from mainline Protestant institutions—churches, denominations, seminaries, mission boards—and strike out on their own, separated from what they reviled as godlessness. Such independence may have been noble, at least according to the standards of fundamentalism, but it was also costly because it meant that the separatists left behind church and school buildings, not to mention endowments. They started from scratch, at considerable expense, and they simply could not afford to be fancy.

The combination of premillennialism and economic stringency may not entirely excuse the architectural atrocities that evangelicals constructed in the twentieth century. It does help to explain them.

★ ★ ★

The theological shift from postmillennial optimism to premillennial pessimism had ripple effects that shaped evangelicalism throughout most of the twentieth century. The evangelical embrace of American society that animated various antebellum reform movements gave way, in the face of profound social and demographic changes, to a deep and brooding suspicion and the expectation of imminent judgment. Evangelicals by the turn of the twentieth century no longer sought to construct a millennial kingdom; that enterprise would have to await divine intervention. Instead, they turned inward, tending to their own piety and seeking to lure others into a spiritualized kingdom in preparation for the imminent return of Jesus.

By adopting dispensational premillennialism, evangelicals ceded the arena of social amelioration to Protestants who had been shaped by the teachings of the Social Gospel. Although they generally avoided the language of postmillennialism, these more liberal Protestants took up the cause of advancing the kingdom of God on earth, even as evangelicals retreated ever more determinedly into their own subculture.

By 1900, the chasm between the liberal Social Gospel and evangelical dispensationalism was firmly established. The very people who had reshaped the nation in the early and middle decades of the nineteenth century now found themselves divided. American Protestantism would never be the same.

3

THE CONSTRUCTION OF A SUBCULTURE
❧

When talking about evangelical attitudes toward society, it is possible, with only modest contrivance, to divide the twentieth century into four equal twenty-five-year periods: 1900–1925, 1925–1950, 1950–1975, and 1975–2000. Within each of these quarters, evangelicals approached the broader culture in very different ways, moving from suspicion and separation during the first half of the twentieth century to engagement and something very close to capitulation in the latter half. Just as social and demographic changes in American society profoundly shaped evangelical theology in the nineteenth century, so too the historical circumstances in each of these eras had broad repercussions on evangelicals and evangelicalism in the twentieth century.

At the dawn of the twentieth century, America's evangelicals were profoundly suspicious of the social changes that had buffeted the United States in the latter half of the nineteenth century. Evangelicals' adoption of dispensational premillennialism in the waning decades of the nineteenth century, with its assurance that Jesus would return at any moment, effectively absolved them from the task of social reform. The social needs of the cities, in any case, were overwhelming and seemed to defy redress. It was better to hunker down, seek the regeneration of other individuals, and scrutinize your own spiritual affairs in preparation for the rapture.

In an odd and somewhat indirect way, evangelicals' embrace of Charles Finney's Arminian theology during the antebellum period exaggerated this tendency. Whereas Wesleyanism and Arminianism empowered individuals to seize control of the salvation process, the corollary was that salvation thus attained could also be imperiled by the failure to live a godly life. Endless theological discussions about "eternal security" among evangelicals (whether or not one's eternal fate had been irreversibly secured at conversion) would have been, if not impossible, at least somewhat less probable among die-hard Calvinists, who taught the "perseverance of the saints," that those whom God had elected for salvation he would preserve to ultimate glorification. Arminians could claim no such assurance of "eternal security," so the task of examining the state of one's soul and devising various devotional exercises to shore up one's spirituality became at least a minor obsession.

With these characteristics—the emphasis on a personalized, introspective faith combined with a general disregard for social reform—evangelicals entered the twentieth century.

* * *

Although no one could have suspected it at the time, nothing reshaped the internal dimensions of evangelicalism in the twentieth century more than the events in Topeka, Kansas, on January 1, 1901, the first day of the new century. Agnes Ozman, a student at Charles Fox Parham's Bethel Bible College, began speaking in tongues after the manner of the early Christians in the second chapter of the Acts of the Apostles. News of this phenomenon spread to other students and, by means of Parham's itinerations, throughout the lower Midwest. William J. Seymour, an African American hotel waiter, carried this pentecostal gospel with him to Los Angeles early in 1906, and *glossolalia* (speaking in tongues) broke out again on April 9 at a house on Bonnie Brae Street, where Parham was staying. Within a week, the fledgling movement relocated to a former warehouse at 312 Azusa Street, and for the next several years the Azusa Street Mission became synonymous with divine healing, pentecostal enthusiasm, and the preparation of missionaries, who fanned out across North America and the world with their pentecostal gospel.

One of the traits of the early years of pentecostalism was its interracial character; Seymour himself was black, and contemporaries noted the absence of racial barriers on Azusa Street. The second notable characteristic was that, like Finney's gatherings in the Second Great Awakening, women were allowed to participate, and some assumed important leadership roles in the early years of pentecostalism. Sadly, those distinctive elements dissipated. As pentecostalism began to organize into institutional forms—the Church of God in Christ, for example, or the Assemblies of God—the denominations were racially homogeneous, even exclusive. Although women were ordained as missionaries and pastors in pentecostal circles in the early decades of pentecostalism, that practice declined over the course of the twentieth century.

Among evangelicals elsewhere, a deepening suspicion began to infect their attitudes toward society. American culture, increasingly urbanized and overrun by immigrants, looked ever more alien. Billy Sunday, a former baseball player for the Chicago White Stockings, railed against the evils of the cities and taunted his auditors to "hit the sawdust trail" and give their lives to Jesus. Another irritant to evangelicals was their uneasy relationship with mainline Protestant denominations, as evidenced by the fundamentalist-modernist controversy. The leaders of Protestantism were departing from Christian orthodoxy, evangelicals charged, by countenancing Charles Darwin's ideas and by compromising on the integrity and inerrancy of the Scriptures. The German discipline of higher criticism, which cast doubts on the authorship of several books of the Bible, had won acceptance in many Protestant seminaries and among too many leaders of mainline Protestant denominations.

Evangelicals issued a full-fledged declaration of war against what they called "modernism" with the publication of a series of pamphlets called *The Fundamentals*. Written by conservative theologians and financed by Lyman and Milton Stewart of Union Oil Company of California, these twelve pamphlets, published between 1910 and 1915, contained conservative defenses of such issues as the virgin birth of Christ, the authenticity of miracles, the inerrancy of the Bible, and the premillennial return of Jesus. Those who subscribed to the doctrines contained therein came to be known as "fundamentalists."

In 1923, J. Gresham Machen, a theologian at Princeton Theological Seminary, published a book entitled *Christianity and Liberalism*. The two, he argued, are fundamentally different, and liberal—or modernist—Protestants should take the honorable course and withdraw from Protestant seminaries and denominations, leaving them to conservatives, the rightful heirs of Protestant orthodoxy.

Liberal Protestants refused to heed Machen's directive, of course, and the era of suspicion that marked evangelicalism in the first quarter of the twentieth century gave way to an era characterized by separation. The career of Machen himself illustrates this transition. Machen became increasingly estranged from his colleagues at Princeton, and his agitation against modernism also angered leaders of the Presbyterian Church. A reorganization of the seminary forced his ouster in 1929, and Machen went on to form an independent missions board, Westminster Theological Seminary, and the Orthodox Presbyterian Church. Similar struggles beset other denominations. Although many conservative evangelicals remained affiliated with mainline congregations and denominations, struggling to effect change or a kind of reclamation, many others bolted to form their own congregations, denominations, and affiliated institutions.

Symbolically, at least, the precipitating event was the famous Scopes trial of 1925. After the Tennessee legislature passed the Butler Act, which forbade the teaching of evolution in the state's public schools, Austin Peay, the governor, signed the measure with the explicit understanding that it would not be enforced. The American Civil Liberties Union had other ideas, placing advertisements in Tennessee newspapers in search of someone to test the constitutionality of such a law. Civic boosters in Dayton, Tennessee, saw an opportunity. They summoned John T. Scopes, a teacher in the local high school, to their gathering at Fred Robinson's drug store, plied him with a fountain drink, and secured his cooperation, even though Scopes could not recall whether or not he had taught evolution when he filled in for the regular biology teacher.

That technicality mattered little, and by the time the combatants assembled in the second story of the Rhea County courthouse for the trial itself, the attention of the entire nation was focused on Dayton, Tennessee. The event drew three of the era's most illustrious men: William Jennings Bryan, the "Great Commoner" and three-time Democratic nominee for president; Clarence Darrow, who had often fought alongside Bryan in various Progressive causes; and H. L. Mencken of the *Baltimore Sun*. Bryan, who assisted in the prosecution of Scopes, had few concerns about Darwinism as a scientific theory; he worried more about the effects of social Darwinism. As the trial unfolded, broadcast live over Chicago radio station WGN, and under the scrutiny of the phalanx of journalists, led by Mencken, Bryan acquitted himself poorly, even though he won his case.

Bryan, and by extension all evangelicals, lost decisively in the larger courtroom of public opinion. Mencken mercilessly lampooned evangelicals and especially Bryan himself, who died suddenly in Dayton five days after the trial. The ignominy surrounding the Scopes trial convinced evangelicals that the larger culture had turned against them. They responded by withdrawing from the culture, which they came to regard as Satan's domain, to construct an alternative universe, an evangelical subculture.

The building that took place among evangelicals in the second quarter of the twentieth century was nothing short of astonishing. They set about forming their own congregations, denominations, missionary societies, publishing houses, Bible institutes, Bible colleges, Bible camps, and seminaries—all in an effort to insulate themselves from the larger world. The project was ambitious and Herculean and costly, but evangelicals believed that the integrity of the faith was at stake. In this era of separation, evangelicals sought to remain unsullied by liberalism, by modernism, or by the world. They withdrew from politics and from any culture outside of their own subculture. That was dictated in part by necessity, by the financial and logistical demands of creating a whole new infrastructure, but it also represented a choice to remain pure.

By the end of the second quarter of the twentieth century, evangelicals had burrowed into their own subculture. They socialized almost entirely within that world, and so comprehensive was this alternative universe that it was possible in the middle decades of the twentieth century (as I can attest personally) to function with virtual autonomy from the larger culture and have, in fact, very little commerce with anyone outside of the evangelical subculture.

★ ★ ★

By mid-century, a few evangelicals thought that the separatist impulse, especially as embodied by such hard-core fundamentalists as Bob Jones and Carl McIntire, had gone too far. Carl F. H. Henry provided a kind of manifesto for the renewed engagement of evangelicals with the larger culture with the publication in 1947 of *The Uneasy Conscience of Modern Fundamentalism*, which argued against the separatism that had become the overriding characteristic of evangelicalism in the second quarter of the twentieth century. The formation of Fuller Theological Seminary the same year that Henry's book appeared provided the so-called neoevangelicals with institutional ballast for their renewed, albeit cautious, engagement with American society in the third quarter of the twentieth century.

As evangelicals tentatively began to emerge from their subculture, they also reclaimed one of the elements of their heritage that had served evangelicalism so well throughout American history: the ability to articulate the vernacular of the culture and to exploit new and emerging communications technologies. No one illustrated this better than Billy Graham, son of a dairy farmer in North

Carolina who became the twentieth century's preeminent religious celebrity.

Like many evangelicals, Graham had been reared in a fundamentalist household, which is to say that he had imbibed the notion that separatism was somehow akin to orthodoxy itself. Graham's one semester at the ultrafundamentalist Bob Jones University, however, apparently soured him somewhat on fundamentalism; he transferred to a Baptist school in Florida and eventually to Wheaton College in Illinois. Graham's considerable gifts as a preacher began to emerge, and early in his career he made a conscious decision to reject fundamentalism in favor of a broader, more inclusive evangelicalism.

The contours of this new understanding of the faith emerged during his revival campaign (which he called a "crusade") in Portland, Oregon, in 1950. In the course of that crusade, Graham made several crucial decisions. First, he decided to incorporate his operation as the Billy Graham Evangelistic Association, thereby adopting a corporate model, which was all the rage at mid-century, and holding himself accountable to a board of directors. In so doing, Graham was able to avoid any hint of financial impropriety—or any other kind of impropriety—throughout a career that extended well beyond a half-century. Graham also decided in Portland to start the *Hour of Decision* radio broadcast, thereby using mass media to advance his message.

The rest is history. Graham's "team" exploited new media technologies brilliantly, and his anticommunist rhetoric in the 1950s drew the attention of several important people, including newspaper magnate William Randolph Hearst and Richard Nixon. Graham's final break with the fundamentalists occurred during his storied nine-week Madison Square Garden crusade in 1957, in the course of which Graham committed the unpardonable sin of enlisting the cooperation of New York City's ministerial alliance, which included some theologically liberal Protestants. The fundamentalists never forgave him.

Graham's willingness to engage the world outside of evangelicalism and his uncanny ability to speak the language of the larger culture set the tone for the third quarter of the twentieth century. With the financial backing of evangelical businessmen, Graham pushed for the formation of a new magazine, *Christianity Today*, in 1956 to counteract the influence of the *Christian Century*, which represented the sentiments of more theologically liberal Protestants. Graham's appearances on the *Tonight Show* and the *Dick Cavett Show* coupled with his very public friendships with a succession of U.S. presidents were enormously, if incalculably, important to evangelicals. Among a beleaguered people who saw themselves as utterly marginal in society, Graham's celebrity allowed them the vicarious satisfaction of feeling somehow less marginal.

Graham's eagerness to engage the culture affected others. Consider the case of a Reformed Church in America minister from Alton, Iowa, who was pastor of the Ivanhoe Reformed Church in Riverside, Illinois. In 1955, Robert Schuller accepted what was essentially a missionary posting to Orange County, California. Very quickly he discerned that this was an automobile culture, so he

rented the Orange Drive-In Theater and distributed leaf-
lets throughout the area inviting the people of southern
California to "Come as you are . . . in the family car."
Schuller perched himself atop the concession stand and
preached to the headlights.

Or consider Chuck Smith in nearby Costa Mesa. In
1965, Smith, a pastor in the International Church of the
Foursquare Gospel, a pentecostal denomination founded in
1927 by Aimee Semple McPherson, accepted the pulpit of
a small congregation of contentious people on the verge
of disbanding. He tapped into the hippie culture of Hun-
tington Beach and turned Calvary Chapel into the beach-
head of the Jesus Movement of the early 1970s and, in so
doing, recast both the music and the worship styles of evangelicalism. On other fronts, several evangelical preachers
exploited changes in the regulations of the Federal Communications Commission to launch their own media empires:
Pat Robertson's Christian Broadcasting Network, Jim Bak-
ker's PTL Network, Paul and Jan Crouch's Trinity Broadcasting Network, as well as countless radio and television
programs. The stage (quite literally) was set for the further
emergence of evangelicals into the broader culture in the
final quarter of the twentieth century.

★ ★ ★

The evangelical strategy of involvement with the larger
culture in the third quarter of the twentieth century prepared evangelicals for a fuller engagement beginning in the
mid-1970s. By then the so-called evangelical resurgence
was well under way, a resurgence that was both real and
illusory. The reemergence of evangelicalism was illusory

in part because of the mainline mirage, the misperception that mainline Protestant denominations were more powerful and influential in the middle decades of the twentieth century than they actually were.

When evangelicals exited mainline denominations beginning in the 1920s, they had formed their own congregations and, to a lesser extent, denominations. Many of the congregations, however, remained independent, unaffiliated with any denomination, a pattern that has been exaggerated with the rise of the megachurches, most of which are not part of any denomination. These circumstances skewed the reporting of membership statistics. Put simply, evangelicals in nondenominational congregations did not show up in aggregate statistics; no denominational agency was reporting their presence. Add to that another peculiarity of theology: like the Puritans of the seventeenth century, many evangelicals demand a public profession of faith in front of the entire congregation before admitting that person to church membership, whereas the criterion for membership in many mainline churches is baptism, often done in infancy. In other words, the real challenge in many mainline churches is getting your name *off* of the membership rolls, while the spiritual standards for evangelical church membership can be intimidating. It is not unusual, then, for a mainline congregation to list a membership of, say, one thousand and have only two hundred show up on a given Sunday, whereas the situation may be exactly the opposite in an evangelical congregation: one thousand on a Sunday, but a membership of only two hundred. (For many years, in fact, Calvary Chapel had no category for membership at all.)

The mainline mirage, then, suggested that mainline Protestants were more numerous and influential than they really were. Beginning in the mid-1960s, however, and continuing more or less to the present, the trajectory of mainline membership, attendance, and giving has been in steady decline. At the same time, evangelicalism has been growing—in numbers, certainly, but more importantly in cultural visibility and influence.

Why did evangelicals emerge so emphatically in the 1970s? The short answer is that the time was ripe. The infrastructure that evangelicals had constructed in earnest following the Scopes trial—colleges, seminaries, publishing houses, media concerns—was now sufficiently established so that it could provide a foundation for evangelicals' return to the public square. More important, American society seemed ready to hear evangelical voices once again. After the Watergate scandal, the ignominy of Vietnam, and the implosion of the counterculture, Americans were ready to hear a new message, a message that cloaked itself in a very simple morality, one that appropriated the language of Christian values.

No politician understood this better than a Southern Baptist Sunday school teacher from Georgia. Jimmy Carter had failed in his first bid for governor, losing to an arch-segregationist, Lester Maddox, in 1966. Carter's defeat prompted a spiritual renewal and then a second gubernatorial run in 1970, this one successful. Almost immediately, Carter began to plot an improbable course that would lead to the Democratic presidential nomination six years later. One of the keynotes of his successful campaign for the White House was that he would "never knowingly lie to the American people."

On the heels of Carter's political success as well as the popularity of *Born Again*, the memoir of Charles Colson, one of the Watergate felons who converted to evangelical Christianity, *Newsweek* magazine declared 1976 "The Year of the Evangelical." That designation turned out to be four years premature; in 1980, all three of the major candidates for president claimed to be born again Christians: Jimmy Carter; Ronald Reagan, the Republican nominee; and John B. Anderson, the Republican-turned-independent who was a member of the Evangelical Free Church of America.

By 1980, however, the evangelical landscape had changed entirely. Carter had lured evangelicals, southerners especially, away from their subculture and out of their apolitical torpor. He did so by speaking the language of evangelicalism; although his declaration that he was a born again Christian sent every journalist in New York to his or her rolodex to figure out what he meant, evangelicals themselves, including Baptists throughout the South, understood perfectly well. He was speaking their language. He was one of them and, more important, unafraid to say so.

One of the great ironies of the twentieth century is that the very people who emerged to help elect Carter in 1976 turned rabidly against him four years later. The rise of the Religious Right as a political entity is something I will address later, but the effects of this political activism have been seismic. Without question, evangelicals have definitely shed their indifference toward temporal matters, plunging into the political process with a vengeance. The ripple effects have been significant. According to pollster Louis Field, had it not been for the participation of politically conservative evangelicals in 1980, many of whom were voting for the first time, Carter would have beaten Reagan by one percent of the popular vote. Since then, in elections from the presidency to the local school board, politically conservative evangelicals have made their presence felt. They have provided for the Republican Party the volunteer efforts that labor unions once supplied for the Democratic Party, thereby altering the American political calculus in the final decades of the twentieth century.

With political success, however, has come compromise, which of course is the way of politics, and this is why I characterize the final quarter of the twentieth century as the era of capitulation on the part of evangelicals to the larger culture. Consider the Reagan years. The televangelist scandals broke in the mid-1980s, and television preachers peddled the so-called prosperity gospel, the notion that the Almighty was itching to bestow the emoluments of middle- and upper-middle-class life on the faithful. The faithful, in turn, were obliged to follow the principles of trickle-down prosperity: send checks to the televangelist and the showers of blessings will rain down on the faithful—after the blessings had first cycled through the rain barrel of the televangelist. The "name it and claim it" doctrine had been present in some evangelical circles as early as the 1940s, but this spiritualized Reaganism flourished as never before in the 1980s.

One of the characteristics of evangelicalism in the middle decades of the twentieth century had been a suspicion of "worldliness," which included a critique of rampant materialism in American society. I remember, as a child, many perorations against the dangers of affluence. Those sermons all but disappeared in the 1980s as evangelicals became quite comfortable indeed with their niche in the suburbs. The premillennial rhetoric of decades past persisted, but no longer with the same enthusiasm or conviction, as upwardly mobile evangelicals settled into middle-class comfort. Yes, Jesus, come again. But take your time; we're doing just fine.

And indeed they were. Megachurches dotted the suburbs. Christian radio and television flooded the airwaves. Political success had bought access to the councils of power. Evangelicalism during the final quarter of the twentieth century was still a subculture—with its distinctive jargon, mores, and celebrities.

But after 1980 or so it was no longer a counterculture.

4

THE RISE OF THE RELIGIOUS RIGHT
✍

By now, well into the twenty-first century, the story of the rise of the Religious Right, the loose coalition of politically conservative individuals, congregations, and organizations, is well known. On January 22, 1973, the United States Supreme Court handed down its landmark *Roe v. Wade* decision that effectively struck down all laws banning abortion until "viability," the point at which a fetus could survive outside the womb. The Roman Catholic Church had been arguing against legalized abortion for a very long time, but sheer outrage at the *Roe* decision had the effect of rallying evangelicals to the antiabortion cause.

For most of the twentieth century, evangelicals had been content to exist within the safety of their subculture, this network of institutions they had constructed in earnest following the Scopes trial of 1925. The subculture functioned as a kind of bulwark against the corruptions of the larger world, and evangelicals' wholesale adoption of dispensational premillennialism late in the previous century effectively exempted them from concerns about social amelioration. Although many evangelicals, including Billy Graham, railed against "godless Communism" during the Cold War, their fixation with the imminent return of Jesus rationalized their lack of interest in the present world. "Believing the Bible as I do," Jerry Falwell declared in 1965, "I would find it impossible to stop preaching the pure saving gospel of Jesus Christ, and begin doing anything else—including fighting Communism, or participating in civil-rights reforms."

Dealing with the victims of systemic discrimination and racist violence was one thing, but protecting those poor, defenseless babies was another. The *Roe* decision of 1973 shook evangelical leaders out of their complacency; even though their own congregants did not want them involved in political matters, the urgency of the *Roe* ruling compelled them to action. They were willing to take on the risk of alienating their own constituencies because of the greater moral imperative of fighting the scourge of abortion.

These leaders of the Religious Right looked for ways to justify their sudden, albeit reluctant, plunge into politics, so they began to refer to themselves as the "new abolitionists," an effort to align themselves with the nineteenth-century opponents of slavery. The political activism on the part of these evangelical leaders was initially viewed with suspicion by rank-and-file evangelicals, but they quickly were persuaded of the moral urgency of fighting abortion.

★ ★ ★

The scenario about the rise of the Religious Right I have just rehearsed is compelling and familiar. It is also a work of fiction. The only factual elements of the preceding story are the 1965 quotation from Jerry Falwell, the self-designated use of the term "new abolitionists," and the Roman Catholic Church's longstanding arguments against abortion. As early as the Iowa precinct caucuses in 1972, the bishops were urging their communicants to support candidates opposed to abortion.

Evangelicals, however, took a very different view of the matter in the early 1970s. Meeting in St. Louis during the summer of 1971, the messengers (delegates) to the Southern Baptist Convention, hardly a redoubt of liberalism, passed a resolution that stated, "we call upon Southern Baptists to work for legislation that will allow the possibility of abortion under such conditions as rape, incest, clear evidence of severe fetal deformity, and carefully ascertained evidence of the likelihood of damage to the emotional, mental, and physical health of the mother." The Southern Baptist Convention reaffirmed that position in 1974 and again in 1976.

After the *Roe* decision was handed down on January 22, 1973, W. A. Criswell, former president of the Southern Baptist Convention and pastor of First Baptist Church in Dallas, Texas, expressed his satisfaction with the ruling. "I have always felt that it was only after a child was born and had a life separate from its mother that it became an individual person," one of the most famous fundamentalists of the twentieth century declared, "and it has always, therefore, seemed to me that what is best for the mother and for the future should be allowed."

While a few evangelical voices, including *Christianity Today* magazine, mildly questioned the ruling, the overwhelming response on the part of evangelicals was silence, even approval; Baptists, in particular, applauded the decision as an appropriate articulation of the line of division between church and state, between personal morality and state regulation of individual behavior. "Religious liberty, human equality and justice are advanced by the Supreme Court abortion decision," W. Barry Garrett of *Baptist Press* wrote.

If the *Roe* decision was not the precipitating cause for the rise of the Religious Right, however, what was? The catalyst for the Religious Right was indeed a court decision, but it was a lower court decision, *Green v. Connally*, not *Roe v. Wade*. In the early 1970s, the federal government was looking for ways to extend the provisions of the Civil Rights Act of 1964, the landmark legislation that Lyndon Johnson pushed through Congress and signed into law during the summer of 1964. The Civil Rights Act forbade racial segregation and discrimination, and in looking for ways to enforce that law the Internal Revenue Service opined that any organization that engaged in racial discrimination was not, by definition, a charitable organization and therefore should be denied tax-exempt status. Furthermore, any contributions to such institutions no longer qualified for tax exemption.

On June 30, 1971, the three-judge District Court for the District of Columbia affirmed the IRS in its *Green v.*

Connally decision. Although *Green v. Connally* addressed the case of a segregated school in Mississippi, the ramifications of the ruling were widespread. Institutions that engaged in racial discrimination, be they churches, clubs, or schools, were no longer tax exempt. As the IRS prepared to apply the ruling, one of the schools directly in its crosshairs was a fundamentalist institution in Greenville, South Carolina: Bob Jones University. Founded in Florida by arch-fundamentalist Bob Jones in 1926, the school had been located for a time in Cleveland, Tennessee, before moving to South Carolina in 1947. In response to *Green v. Connally*, Bob Jones University decided to admit students of color in 1971, but, out of fears of miscegenation, the school maintained its restrictions against admitting unmarried African Americans until 1975. Even then, however, the school stipulated that interracial dating would be grounds for expulsion, and the school also promised that any students who "espouse, promote, or encourage others to violate the University's dating rules and regulations will be expelled."

The IRS pressed its case against Bob Jones University and on April 16, 1975, notified the school of the proposed revocation of its tax-exempt status. On January 19, 1976, the IRS officially revoked Bob Jones University's tax-exempt status, effective retroactively to 1970, when the school had first been formally notified of the IRS policy.

Bob Jones University sued to retain its tax exemption, and conservative activist Paul Weyrich saw an opening. Weyrich had been fighting for conservative causes going back to Barry Goldwater's failed bid for the presidency in 1964. He sensed the electoral potential of enlisting evangelical voters in the conservative crusade, and he had been trying throughout the early 1970s to generate some interest from evangelical leaders on matters like abortion, school prayer, pornography, and the proposed equal rights amendment to the U.S. Constitution. "I was trying to get those people interested in those issues and I utterly failed," Weyrich recalled in the 1990s. "What changed their mind was Jimmy Carter's intervention against Christian schools, trying to deny them tax-exempt status on the basis of so-called de facto segregation."

★ ★ ★

The Bob Jones case caught the attention of evangelical leaders, although I do not believe that the primary motivation for the galvanization of evangelicals was racism. Rather, they saw themselves as defending what they considered the sanctity of the evangelical subculture from outside interference. As I was growing up in evangelicalism in the 1950s and 1960s, I recall the visits of a succession of presidents of various Bible colleges and Bible institutes. They were raising money and recruiting students, and one of their mantras was that their institutions did not accept federal money; therefore, the government could not tell them how to run their shops, who they could admit or reject, who they must hire or fire.

Green v. Connally changed that. Evangelical leaders, prodded by Weyrich, chose to interpret the IRS ruling against segregationist schools as an assault on the integrity and the sanctity of the evangelical subculture. And that is what prompted them to action and to organize into a political movement. "What caused the movement to surface,"

Weyrich reiterated, "was the federal government's moves against Christian schools," which, he added, "enraged the Christian community." Ed Dobson, formerly Falwell's assistant at Moral Majority, has corroborated Weyrich's account. "The Religious New Right did not start because of a concern about abortion," he said in 1990. "I sat in the non-smoke-filled back room with the Moral Majority, and I frankly do not remember abortion being mentioned as a reason why we ought to do something."

The Bob Jones case progressed all the way to the Supreme Court in 1982, when the Reagan administration argued on behalf of Bob Jones University. On May 24, 1983, however, the Court ruled 8-to-1 against Bob Jones; the sole dissenter was William Rehnquist, whom Reagan later elevated to chief justice of the Supreme Court. The evangelical defense of Bob Jones University and its racially discriminatory policies may not have been motivated primarily by racism, and I do not think it was. Still, it is fair to point out the paradox that the very people who style themselves the "new abolitionists" to emphasize their moral kinship with the nineteenth-century opponents of slavery actually coalesced as a political movement effectively to defend racial discrimination.

And how did opposition to abortion become part of the Religious Right's program? According to Weyrich, once these evangelical leaders had mobilized in defense of Bob Jones University, they held a conference call to discuss the possibility of other political activities. Several people suggested potential issues, and finally a voice on the end of one of the lines said, "How about abortion?"

And that, according to Weyrich, was how abortion was cobbled into the agenda of the Religious Right—in the late 1970s, not as a direct response to the January 1973 *Roe v. Wade* decision.

★ ★ ★

Another element of Paul Weyrich's statement merits closer examination. Looking back on the formation of the Religious Right, Weyrich insisted that opposition to abortion was not the precipitating cause behind evangelical political activism. His alternate explanation reads as follows: "What changed their mind was Jimmy Carter's intervention against Christian schools, trying to deny them tax-exempt status on the basis of so-called de facto segregation."

Here, Weyrich displays his genius for political maneuvering and chicanery. The IRS had initiated its action against Bob Jones University in 1970, and they informed the school in 1975 that they would revoke its tax exemption. Jimmy Carter was still running for the Democratic nomination when Bob Jones University received that news, and he was inaugurated as president on January 20, 1977, precisely one full year and a day *after* the IRS finally rescinded the school's tax-exempt status. And yet, according to Weyrich, it was "Jimmy Carter's intervention against Christian schools" that precipitated the rise of the Religious Right.

As president of the United States in the final years of the 1970s, Carter was dealt a bad hand—the Arab Oil Embargo and the concomitant energy crisis, high interest rates, the Iranian hostage situation—and it is a hand that, in many respects, he played badly. But he also fought

against some lavishly funded, highly organized, and fiend-
ishly deceptive opponents who would do almost anything
to undermine him. Weyrich's attribution to Carter of the
IRS action against Bob Jones University provides a case in
point. Even though the action was consummated a full year
before Carter even took office, when Gerald Ford was still
president, Weyrich succeeded in pinning this unpopular
action on the Democratic president and using it to organize a movement to deny him reelection in 1980.

One of the many ironies surrounding the Religious
Right, of course, is that evangelicals had helped sweep
Carter to victory in the presidential election of 1976. His
rhetoric about being a "born again Christian" had energized
evangelicals, many of whom had been resolutely apolitical until the mid-1970s. His improbable run for the presidency, his candor about his religious convictions, and his
promise to restore probity to the White House resonated
with many Americans, especially after having endured
Richard Nixon's endless prevarications. But no group
responded more enthusiastically than evangelicals themselves. Many of them registered to vote for the first time
in order to cast their ballots for the Sunday school teacher
from Plains, Georgia, and even televangelist Pat Robertson
later boasted that he had done everything short of violating
FCC regulations to ensure Carter's election.

Not all evangelicals were enthusiastic about Carter,
however. Tim LaHaye insisted that he had been suspicious from the beginning. Once they had galvanized as a
political movement, leaders of the Religious Right claimed
that Carter's unwillingness to outlaw abortion provided a

compelling reason to work against him—Carter had taken the position during the 1976 campaign that he was "personally opposed" to abortion but that he did not want to make it illegal—but that was a retrospective judgment because evangelicals did not embrace abortion as an issue until the late 1970s, in preparation for the 1980 campaign.

What about other issues that fed the rise of the Religious Right? Phyllis Schlafly, a Roman Catholic, had been opposing the proposed equal rights amendment to the U.S. Constitution, but the issue had little traction among evangelicals in the early 1970s. As the Religious Right was gearing up for the 1980 election, however, Beverly LaHaye started a new organization, Concerned Women for America, in 1979, claiming that she resented the assumption on the part of feminist leaders that they spoke for all women.

The decision by the Religious Right to oppose feminism as part of their agenda was a curious one. Following the lead of Charles Finney, Phoebe Palmer, Sarah Lankford, and countless Quaker women, evangelicals had been in the forefront of the women's rights movement throughout the nineteenth century and into the twentieth century. An essential part of the case for women's suffrage was that women could bring moral arguments to bear on social issues, especially temperance. Given their own legacy, evangelical women should have been marching beside people like Gloria Steinem and Betty Friedan in the women's movement of the 1960s and 1970s, and one can only speculate about the ways in which America might have looked different in the final decades of the twentieth century had they done so. At the very least, it seems likely that an evangelical presence in the women's movement might have curbed some of the more radical elements of feminism. But that, of course, is speculation. Instead, the leaders of the Religious Right, who were and are overwhelmingly male, opposed the women's movement, thereby betraying evangelicalism's own heritage as nineteenth-century feminists.

★ ★ ★

In their search for a comprehensive political agenda, the leaders of the Religious Right grabbed onto such issues as support for Israel, derived from their millennialist reading of biblical prophecies, and the abolition of the federal department of education. But in establishing a social agenda, which they insisted was based directly on the teachings of scripture, they ignored the issue of divorce in favor of opposition to abortion and, later, homosexuality.

On the face of it, this was a curious move. The Bible, not to mention Jesus himself, says a great deal about divorce—and none of it good. The Bible says relatively little about homosexuality and probably nothing at all about abortion, though pro-life advocates routinely cite a couple of verses. Jesus himself said nothing whatsoever about sexuality, though he did talk a good bit about money. Still, the preponderance of the biblical witness, which the Religious Right claims as formative, is directed toward the believer's responsibility to those Jesus calls "the least of these," toward an honoring of the meek and peacemakers, and, on social matters, against divorce. Yet the Religious Right made no attempt to outlaw divorce.

Why is that? First, the divorce rate among evangelicals by the late 1970s, when the Religious Right was gearing up, was roughly the same as that of the larger population. Second, the person that the Religious Right anointed as their political savior in 1980 was Ronald Reagan, a divorced and remarried man who, as governor of California, had signed a bill into law legalizing abortion. The Religious Right's designation of abortion and homosexuality as the central issues of their social agenda allowed them to divert attention from their embrace of Reagan but also to locate "sin" outside of the evangelical subculture (or so they thought).

This attempt to externalize the enemy proved effective. By the logic of their own professed fidelity to the Scriptures, the leaders of the Religious Right should have been working to make divorce illegal, except in cases of infidelity. Not more difficult, but illegal, because they seek to outlaw abortion. Instead, they have chosen to be draconian on abortion and homosexuality, even though the biblical mandate on those matters is considerably more ambiguous. The Religious Right's opposition to abortion has been weakened, moreover, by its insistent refusal to be consistently "pro-life." Unlike the Roman Catholic Church, which, following the lead of the late Joseph Cardinal Bernardin, archbishop of Chicago, has talked about a "consistent life ethic," the leaders of the Religious Right have failed to condemn capital punishment or even the use of torture by the Bush administration.

The failure to oppose capital punishment and torture leaves the Religious Right open to the charge that their agenda is driven by hard-right ideologues rather than by moral conviction. And what do we make of the fact that the Republican-Religious Right coalition controlled all three branches of the federal government from February 1, 2006, when Samuel Alito was sworn in to the Supreme Court, until January 3, 2007, when the new Democratic majorities took control of Congress? During those eleven months, the chief executive, the majority leader of the Senate, and the speaker of the House of Representatives all claimed to be evangelical Christians and unalterably opposed to abortion. Yet they made no attempt whatsoever to outlaw abortion, their stated goal. They did, however, pass and sign into law the Military Commissions Act in October 2006, which sought to legitimize the use of torture.

* * *

Despite the internal contradictions and ironies surrounding the Religious Right, no one can deny its political effectiveness. The Religious Right more than likely provided the margin of victory for Reagan in 1980 over two evangelical opponents: Carter, the incumbent, and John B. Anderson, Republican member of Congress from Illinois who was running as an independent. The Religious Right helped to reelect Reagan four years later and to elect Reagan's vice president, George H. W. Bush, in 1988, even though the support from politically conservative evangelicals was considerably more tepid. Leaders of the Religious Right viewed the Clinton years as something of an interregnum; as someone shaped by the Baptist tradition in the South and as someone clearly at ease behind the pulpit of an African American congregation, Clinton was able to siphon enough evangelical votes away from the Republicans to win election in 1992 and reelection four years later.

The leaders of the Religious Right never forgave Clinton for interrupting their ascendancy. With the emergence of the Monica Lewinsky scandal, they pounced with a vengeance, and their failure to remove him from office by impeachment was a source of unmitigated disappointment. They finally had Clinton in their sights, but the Senate failed to pull the trigger, despite the Republican majority. Ed Dobson and Cal Thomas, both of them former assistants to Jerry Falwell, published a bitter lamentation about the betrayal of the Religious Right by the political process. Their book, *Blinded by Might: Can the Religious Right Save America?*, answered the subtitle with an emphatic no. Politics, they argued, was an arena of compromise, not suited to religious convictions. Besides, what had the Republican Party actually delivered to politically conservative evangelicals?

A fair question. No one can deny the political influence of the Religious Right or the leaders' proximity to powerful politicians. Since the 1980s, politically conservative evangelicals have supplied the Republican Party with the foot soldiers that labor unions once provided for the Democratic Party. But what have evangelicals received in return?

Both Reagan and George H. W. Bush (who had run for the Republican presidential nomination in 1980 as a pro-choice Republican) promised a constitutional amendment banning abortion, but neither made a serious effort to amend the Constitution. Reagan appointed C. Everett Koop, an evangelical and an abortion opponent, to the position of surgeon general, and Gary Bauer held a policy position in the Reagan White House. But the legislative accomplishments of the Religious Right, despite the putative allegiance of a majority of Congress to the agenda of the Religious Right, are negligible. Even George W. Bush's much-trumpeted faith-based initiatives program fell far short of his promises. According to *Tempting Faith: An Inside Story of Political Seduction* by David Kuo, formerly the assistant in Bush's office of faith-based initiatives, Bush delivered only $80 million of the $8 billion dollars he promised to the program, less than one percent. "In 2004 we really did break our necks to turn out the vote," James Dobson complained in September 2006. "For the two years since then, I have been extremely disappointed with what the Republicans have done with the power they were given."

★ ★ ★

The rise of the Religious Right in the late 1970s and its pandering to power provide an important lesson about evangelicalism. The widespread attempts on the part of the Religious Right to compromise the First Amendment—by means of faith-based initiatives, public prayer in public schools, the use of taxpayer vouchers for religious schools, emblazoning the Ten Commandments and other religious sentiments on public places—all of these efforts ultimately undermine the faith by identifying it with the state and by suggesting that the faith needs the imprimatur of the government for legitimacy. After Judge Myron Thompson ruled (correctly) that the granite monument placed by Roy Moore in the lobby of the Alabama Judicial Building represented a violation of the First Amendment's establishment clause, one of the protesters screamed, "Get your hands off my God!" This protester may have forgotten that one of the commandments etched into that block of granite said something about graven images, but the entire incident illustrated the dangers of trivializing or fetishizing the faith by associating it with the state. The overwhelming lesson of American religious history is that religion, especially evangelicalism, has flourished here as nowhere else precisely because we have followed Roger Williams's dictum that the church should remain separate from the state, lest the "garden of the church" be overcome by the "wilderness of the world."

The other lesson for evangelicals in American religious history is that religion always functions best at the margins of society and not in the councils of power. Methodism in the nineteenth century comes to mind, as do Mormonism and the holiness movement. In the twentieth century, pentecostalism provides the best example of a religious movement operating at the fringes of society— and flourishing. When the faith hankers after political power or cultural respectability, however, it loses its prophetic edge. The failure of the Religious Right to condemn the Bush administration's policies on torture provides perhaps the most egregious example. But twentieth-century American history provides another example as well: the white-middle-class aspirations of mainline Protestants and the ecumenical movement in the Cold War era that led to an enervation of mainline Protestantism. Paradoxically, it was the resurgence of evangelicalism, coming from the margins, that re-energized Protestantism. Now, because of the Religious Right's dalliance with the Republican

Party in the decades surrounding the turn of the twentieth century, it is evangelicalism itself that stands in need
of renewal.

And there is evidence that this is already taking place.
Midway through George W. Bush's second term in office,
in the face of economic stagnation, policies that overwhelmingly favored the affluent, indifference toward the
poor and the environment, and moral malpractice in the
use of torture and the conduct of the war in Iraq, evangelical voices began to rise in opposition, calling evangelicalism to its better self. Evangelicals like Jim Wallis and Tony
Campolo were finally being heard, and a new group calling
itself "Red Letter Christians," a reference to the words of
Jesus in many editions of the New Testament, organized in
September 2006 to offer an alternative evangelical voice.
Indeed, history may very well judge the ascendancy of the
Religious Right in the final decades of the twentieth cen-
tury as an aberration because of its distortion of the New
Testament and its failure to honor the legacy of nineteenth-
century evangelical activists.

Because of its malleability, its populism, and its uncanny
knack for speaking the language of the culture, evangelicalism will continue to be America's folk religion well into
the twenty-first century. The mechanisms for course cor-
rections are inherent to evangelicalism, which has always
remained remarkably free of the institutional machinery of
episcopacy, creed, tradition, and denominational bureau-
cracy. And the unparalleled ability to communicate to the
masses, from the open-air preaching of George Whitefield
in the eighteenth century to the stadium crusades of Billy

Graham in the twentieth century, has always ensured that evangelicalism remains accessible to all Americans.

★ ★ ★

The history of evangelicalism in America reveals its suppleness, its infinite adaptability to cultural circumstances. The adoption of a novel configuration of church and state in the seventeenth and eighteenth centuries provides one example, and the theological shift from Calvinism to Arminianism in the new nation provides another. The move from postmillennialism to premillennialism may have had the unfortunate effect of removing evangelicals from the arena of social amelioration, but it was an understandable response to the seismic social and demographic shifts of the nineteenth century. Evangelicals responded to the fundamentalist-modernist controversy and to the Scopes trial by constructing and burrowing into their own subculture, and the rise of the Religious Right in the late 1970s represented a response to the perceived attacks on the sanctity of the subculture. The attempt on the part of the leaders of the Religious Right to obfuscate the real origins of the movement, however, suggests a level of deception that should be disturbing to any believer. The effect of the Religious Right has been to deliver the faith into the captivity of right-wing politics.

Evangelicalism has profoundly shaped American history and culture. The challenge facing evangelicals now, in the early years of the twenty-first century, lies in finding a way to reclaim the faith from the depredations and distortions of the Religious Right.

CONCLUSION

❧

For several years now, in lectures, essays, and books, I
have tried to make the case that the most effective and
successful religious movements in American history have
always situated themselves on the margins of society, not
in the councils of power. The Methodists of the nineteenth
century come to mind, and even the Mormons. For most
of the twentieth century, pentecostalism fit that descrip-
tion. By contrast, anytime a religious group hankers after
political power or cultural influence, in my judgment, it
loses its prophetic voice. The civil rights movement of the
1950s and 1960s provides perhaps the best example of
how to retain a critical distance. Martin Luther King Jr.
enlisted the cooperation of Lyndon Johnson in the passage
of the landmark Civil Rights Act of 1964 and the Voting
Rights Act of 1965. Yet King refused to allow access to

power to compromise his moral judgment. On April 4, 1967, not quite two years after the Voting Rights Act, King ascended the pulpit at Riverside Church in New York City and unleashed a thunderous denunciation of Johnson's war in Vietnam. "A nation that continues year after year to spend more money on military defense than on programs of social uplift," King warned, "is approaching spiritual death."

Evangelicalism over the last several decades, and certainly during the first eight years of the twenty-first century, illustrates copiously the dangers of lusting after political power and cultural influence. In the mid-1970s, evangelicals emerged from their subculture with a vengeance, seeking to make their presence felt in the media, in culture, and in politics. On the face of it, those efforts were wildly successful. Evangelicals made their mark on television, radio, and the music industry; spawned megachurches throughout the nation; and helped to elect Republican politicians to office, from school boards to the presidency.

But at what cost? Evangelicals allowed themselves to be co-opted by powerful political interests. Many evangelicals voted reflexively for any Republican candidate running for office, and evangelicals became the core constituency of the Republican Party. *Christianity Today*, the magazine that considers itself the flagship of evangelical publications, has lost few opportunities over the past decade to gush over any Republican politician who would submit to an interview—including such avatars of "family values" as the thrice-married Newt Gingrich. For thirty years, the Religious Right's singular focus on abortion and homosexuality blinded evangelicals to other moral issues: poverty, AIDS, global warming, and the invasion of Iraq, which met none of the just-war criteria that have been present in Christian thinking for centuries: Is it a defensive war? Have all other options been exhausted? Is there a reasonable chance of success? Is the amount of military force roughly proportional to the provocation? Have measures been taken, as much as possible, to shield civilians from collateral damage?

When I was writing *Thy Kingdom Come* several years back, I asked eight Religious Right organizations to send me a copy of their group's position on the use of torture. Only two of the eight responded, and neither could bring itself to condemn the Bush administration's persistent and systematic use of torture. The very people who purport to hear a fetal scream turned a deaf ear to the real screams of fully formed human beings who were being tortured in the name of our government. And am I the only one who finds it a tad ironic that the same folks who sought to teach something called "intelligent design" in public-school classrooms seemed to evince precious little interest in the handiwork of the Intelligent Designer?

Columns of the faithful (including family members) regularly excoriate me when they learn that I rarely vote Republican. How can I call myself a Christian, they ask, much less an evangelical? For too many years I offered an exasperated defense, arguing that the Bible I read enjoins me to act with justice and points me toward the left of the political spectrum. More recently, however, I turn the question around and ask my accusers to explain to me how the right-wing policies of recent years are in any way consistent with the teachings of Jesus, who expressed concern for the tiniest sparrow and who invited his followers to be peacemakers, to love their enemies, to care for "the least of these."

Silence generally ensues, or at best some prolonged sputtering.

★   ★   ★

The 2008 presidential election laid the groundwork for yet another turning point in American evangelicalism. For the first time in recent memory, perhaps since Jimmy Carter, the Democratic nominee was more comfortable talking about his faith than the Republican nominee, who could not seem to decide whether he was a Baptist or an Episcopalian. Other factors contributed to this shift of evangelicals away from lockstep allegiance to the Republican Party: a generational divide among evangelicals, with younger evangelicals recognizing the importance of environmental matters and showing little interest in the issue of sexual identity; the absence of a viable Republican candidate with strong ties to evangelicalism; general, widespread dissatisfaction with the policies of the George W. Bush administration; a growing conviction among evangelicals that the spectrum of "moral issues" extends well beyond abortion and homosexuality.

In addition, the high-profile stumbles of several figures associated with the Religious Right served further to undermine the movement's credibility: Ted Haggard, former megachurch pastor and president of the National

Association of Evangelicals, who confessed to liaisons with a male prostitute; Larry Craig, former senator from Idaho, he of the "wide stance" in a Minnesota men's room; David Vitter, senator from Louisiana and professed evangelical, who frequented brothels in Washington and New Orleans; and Randy "Duke" Cunningham, now serving a federal prison sentence for corruption, who earned a one hundred percent rating from the Christian Coalition when he represented San Diego as a member of Congress.

Some of the reasons for the demise of the Religious Right are more germane to this discussion than others, and the purpose here is not to point fingers or to assign blame. The moral lapses of the Bush administration alone should have been sufficient to shake evangelical confidence in the political process, or at least to alert them to the dangers of aligning solely with a particular political party. Put simply, the Religious Right finally collapsed beneath the weight of its own contradictions—and that presents evangelicals with an opportunity to set things aright and choose a different course.

* * *

As a historian, I believe that any look toward the future should begin with a glance back at the past. Beyond the cautionary tale of the Religious Right, evangelicals can look deeper into their history to find a better vision for the future. Antebellum evangelicalism, in my judgment, offers a salutary model. Evangelicals early in the nineteenth century sought to reform society in an effort to bring about the kingdom of God here on earth. They worked for the abolition of slavery and for the formation of common schools (known today as public schools) in order to provide a better life and at least a measure of upward mobility to those who were disadvantaged. They recognized the perils of alcohol abuse and organized the temperance movement. They wanted to rehabilitate, not merely to incarcerate, criminals ("penitentiary"). They sought equal rights for women, including voting rights.

These evangelicals overreached at times, and some of their efforts seem suffocating and paternalistic by today's standards. Nor did they always avoid the pitfalls of religious or ethnic bigotry. But they invariably took the part of those on the margins of society—women, African Americans, victims of abuse, the poor—a predilection that I find lacking in the actions and agenda of the Religious Right.

I envision an evangelicalism for the twenty-first century that takes seriously the words of the Hebrew prophets who called for justice, an evangelicalism that honors the teachings and the example of Jesus, who asked his followers to act as peacemakers and to care for "the least of these." Such an evangelicalism, I am confident, would look rather different from that of recent years.

The past continues to warn against the seductions of power and influence. Evangelicals, though no longer mired in their subculture with its attendant dangers of insularity, must position themselves once again at the margins of society. This, after all, is where Jesus conducted his earthly ministry, and it is also where nineteenth-century evangelicals were most effective. I am not arguing here that voices of faith should not make themselves heard in the arena of public discourse. Not at all. I happen to think that public discourse would be impoverished without those voices. But we who aspire to be the followers of Jesus must never confuse political access with prophetic witness.

And we must be wary, too, of the blandishments of the culture. When I was growing up as an evangelical in the 1950s and 1960s, the most damning thing you could say about a fellow believer was that she was "worldly." The term *worldliness* had many connotations—enslavement to fashion, sexual promiscuity, dissolute lifestyle—but it also included a strong suspicion of affluence. I heard a lot of sermons in my youth about the perils of wealth and about camels trying to negotiate the eyes of needles. I have not heard one in decades.

Sifting through the evangelical past suggests that there are dangers aplenty in too great a segregation from society, as in the "premillennial" years beginning late in the nineteenth century and during the era of the evangelical subculture in the middle decades of the twentieth century. But I wonder if there is not a reciprocal danger of utter permeability to cultural currents, especially in attitudes toward affluence. Is it any wonder that the so-called "prosperity theology," a kind of spiritualized Reaganism, flourished among evangelicals during the 1980s?

★　★　★

The past is behind us, and there is not a whole lot we can do to change it. In the words of the *New Zealand Prayer Book*, "What has been done has been done / what has not been done has not been done / let it be."

But the real value of historical understanding is that we can learn from the past and use its lessons to chart a better future. Evangelicals now stand at the cusp of that future, another turning point, a critical juncture. We can continue the narrow, petrified policies of the recent past. Or we can chart a new course, one that more fully embraces both the teachings of Jesus as well as the best of evangelicalism's history.

These are the two roads that diverge in Robert Frost's woods.

SUGGESTED READINGS

Ammerman, Nancy Tatom. *Bible Believers: Fundamentalists in the Modern World*. New Brunswick, N.J.: Rutgers University Press, 1987.

Balmer, Randall. *God in the White House: How Faith Shaped the Presidency from John F. Kennedy to George W. Bush*. San Francisco: HarperOne, 2008.

———. *Mine Eyes Have Seen the Glory: A Journey into the Evangelical Subculture in America*. 4th ed. New York: Oxford University Press, 2006.

———. *Thy Kingdom Come: How the Religious Right Distorts the Faith and Threatens America*. New York: Basic Books, 2006.

Blumhofer, Edith L. *Restoring the Faith: The Assemblies of God, Pentecostalism, and American Culture*. Urbana: University of Illinois Press, 1993.

Boles, John B. *The Great Revival, 1787–1805: The Origins of the Southern Evangelical Mind*. Lexington: University Press of Kentucky, 1982.

Boyer, Paul. *When Time Shall Be No More: Prophecy Belief in Modern American Culture*. Cambridge, Mass.: Harvard University Press, 1992.

Butler, Jon. *Awash in a Sea of Faith: Christianizing the American People*. Cambridge, Mass.: Harvard University Press, 1990.

Carpenter, Joel A. *Revive Us Again: The Reawakening of American Fundamentalism*. New York: Oxford University Press, 1997.

Chappell, David L. *A Stone of Hope: Prophetic Religion and the Death of Jim Crow*. Chapel Hill: University of North Carolina Press, 2004.

Dayton, Donald W. *Discovering an Evangelical Heritage*. New York: Harper & Row, 1976.

Frykholm, Amy Johnson. *Rapture Culture: Left Behind in Evangelical America*. New York: Oxford University Press, 2007.

Gaustad, Edwin S. *Faith of the Founders: Religion and the New Nation, 1776–1826*. Waco, Tex.: Baylor University Press, 2004.

Griffith, R. Marie. *God's Daughters: Evangelical Women and the Power of Submission*. Berkeley: University of California Press, 2000.

Hambrick-Stowe, Charles E. *Charles G. Finney and the Spirit of American Evangelicalism*. Grand Rapids: Eerdmans, 1996.

Hatch, Nathan O. *The Democratization of American Christianity*. New Haven: Yale University Press, 1989.

Hempton, David. *Methodism: Empire of the Spirit*. New Haven: Yale University Press, 2005.

Heyrman, Christine Leigh. *Southern Cross: The Beginnings of the Bible Belt*. New York: Alfred E. Knopf, 1997.

Johnson, Paul E. *A Shopkeeper's Millennium: Society and Revivals in Rochester, New York, 1815–1837*. New York: Hill & Wang, 2004.

Kidd, Thomas S. *The Great Awakening: The Roots of Evangelical Christianity in Colonial America*. New Haven: Yale University Press, 2007.

Lambert, Frank. *Religion in American Politics: A Short History*. Princeton, N.J.: Princeton University Press, 2008.

Magnuson, Norris. *Salvation in the Slums: Evangelical Social Work, 1865–1920*. Lanham, Md.: Scarecrow Press, 1977.

Marsden, George M. *Fundamentalism and American Culture*. 2nd ed. New York: Oxford University Press, 2006.

————. *Jonathan Edwards: A Life*. New Haven: Yale University Press, 2003.

————. *Reforming Fundamentalism: Fuller Seminary and the New Evangelicalism*. Grand Rapids: Eerdmans, 1987.

————. *Understanding Fundamentalism and Evangelicalism*. Grand Rapids: Eerdmans, 1991.

Martin, William. *A Prophet with Honor: The Billy Graham Story*. New York: Morrow, 1991.

————. *With God on Our Side: The Rise of the Religious Right in America*. New York: Broadway Books, 1996.

Noll, Mark A. *The Rise of Evangelicalism: The Age of Edwards, Whitefield, and the Wesleys*. Downers Grove, Ill.: InterVarsity, 2004.

Sandeen, Ernest R. *The Roots of Fundamentalism: British and American Millenarianism, 1800–1930*. Chicago: University of Chicago Press, 1970.

Schmidt, Leigh Eric. *Holy Fairs: Scotland and the Making of American Revivalism*. 2nd ed. Grand Rapids: Eerdmans, 2001.

Stephens, Randall J. *The Fire Spreads: Holiness and Pentecostalism in the American South*. Cambridge, Mass.: Harvard University Press, 2008.

Stout, Harry S. *The Divine Dramatist: George Whitefield and the Rise of American Evangelicalism.* Grand Rapids: Eerdmans, 1991.

————. *Upon the Altar of the Nation: A Moral History of the Civil War.* New York: Viking, 2006.

Wacker, Grant. *Heaven Below: Early Pentecostals and American Culture.* Cambridge, Mass.: Harvard University Press, 2001.

Wigger, John H. *Taking Heaven by Storm: Methodism and the Rise of Popular Christianity in America.* New York: Oxford University Press, 1998.